LEADER ON THE
PITCH

Scott Quinnell   Paul Boross

CGW
PUBLISHING

2017

Leader on the Pitch

First Edition: August 2017

ISBN 978-1-9082934-1-1

Published by:

CGW Publishing
B 1502
PO Box 15113
Birmingham
B2 2NJ
United Kingdom

www.cgwpublishing.com

ACKNOWLEDGEMENTS

I would like to express my gratitude to everyone who has helped me throughout my career in rugby and on television.

I would like to thank all the players and coaches I have played with throughout my career and all the people in television who have always been so generous with their support and advice.

Thanks to the international rugby family who I feel proud to be part of and will never take for granted.

Above all I want to thank my family who have been there for me and with me every step of the way. Finally, very special thanks to Nicola, Lucy, Samantha and Steel. I love you so much.

Scott

There are a few people who I would like to acknowledge and give a huge 'thank you' to for their part in the creation of this book.

Sam and Henrietta – I love you – thank you for your constant support and inspiration.

Sam - watching you grow into a charming and talented young man has taught me so much and you still inspire me to learn more.

My parents Laszlo and Helen, for their love and support and for teaching me the values that have held me in good stead throughout my life.

David Rose for the fabulous photos and multi media support.

Stuart and Sue Pearson for their excellent design input.

Our publisher Christopher Greenaway and everyone at CGW publishing for their continued professionalism and support.

Emma Hughes for the superb and subtle photo retouching.

The colleagues and friends who have inspired and influenced me; especially Brian Colbert, Kate Benson and Dr Tim O'Brien. Also, much respect and thanks to Dr Richard Bandler, John and Kathleen LaValle and the Society of NLP.

Paul

FOREWORD

The philosophy that I've held for many years is to "think different". It's a philosophy that helped me to lead the England Rugby team to a memorable victory, but what's more important is that it's a philosophy which has served me throughout my life and my business career.

Of course, it's not always enough to think different, we have to know what to think about, and our thoughts have to lead us into action.

As with any game, Rugby is a combination of strategy and action. You have to understand yourself and your team, and you have to consider what the other team are planning. But once you're on the pitch, the time for planning is over, and there's no time to stop and think about whether you're right or wrong, you just have to go with it and find a way to make it work.

As a metaphor for business, Rugby really stands out to me. Few other sports carry the unique challenges of Rugby, including the ever-present threat of physical injury. In business, the threat of failure equally causes leaders to lose their composure and make hasty decisions, and the end result isn't because the decision was wrong but because it was made under pressure.

Any resource that helps you to think clearly under pressure is invaluable, and if you don't have the luxury of a lifetime's experience of overcoming setbacks then a great way to start is by learning from people who've been there before you. In the end, you can't get away from the need to learn from your own mistakes, but that learning comes much faster and easier when you are open to the lessons that others can share with you.

When I speak to business people, one of the things I advise them on is the use of 'critical non-essentials', the things that don't obviously seem essential to what you're doing but which make a critical difference to your attitude, your relationships and your results. Such ideas helped me to build successful teams in both Rugby and in business, and I've really learned what a huge difference such things can make.

This book is one of those critical non-essentials. Read it, re-read it, and allow yourself to learn from the deeper wisdom of the game.

Sir Clive Woodward

LEADER ON THE PITCH

Leadership and rugby. You might be thinking that you know where this is heading. Countless retired sports professionals turned leadership gurus have written and spoken about leadership. Leading from the front. Motivating a team. Inspiring people to give their best. You've heard it all before.

So what can we possibly add to the subject? A TV and business psychologist and an international rugby captain?

Well, I'm not going to sell it to you. You can read this book or not. You can pay attention to our experiences and stories or not. You can make a difference to the lives of the people you lead or not. Because ultimately, that's what leadership is really about – making choices.

We each make choices every day, whether to get up and go to work, what to have for lunch, what to do in the evening. Most of the choices that you make affect you, and maybe a handful of people around you. Take a parking space, now it's unavailable for someone else. Take a job, now your family are affected by your working hours. These are well defined choices, contained, constrained.

Imagine making a choice which affects not only you but dozens, or hundreds, or thousands, or millions of people. How do you deal with that? And how do you live with the consequences?

In a game of rugby, what's the worst that can happen? A bloody nose? A few bruises? A broken bone? A lost game? Go to any rugby match, or any sporting event, and you'll quickly discover that sport isn't just about the game, it's about the struggle that the game represents. The struggle over the opposing team? Maybe. But the struggle over your own doubts and fears is far more significant, and far more risky. A moment's hesitation could lead to an injury which ends a career. Maybe the game of business is played at a slower pace yet the stakes are just as high.

Rugby and business are not games played against competitors. The other team merely sets the boundaries for the game. They merely punish your mistakes. They show you the chasm that opens when your doubts take hold. They show you the path to what you could become.

The real competitor is yourself.

In this book, we are going to share the lessons we've learned through both of our long and varied careers, on and off the pitch, and many series of the TV show 'School of Hard Knocks', and we're going to translate those lessons into your language, the language of leadership. Because if your choices aren't changing the world, you're not playing hard enough.

If your choices aren't changing the world, you're not playing hard enough

WHAT IS LEADERSHIP?

We all know what leadership is, don't we? It's the person standing on the side line, urging a team onwards. It's the person on the stage, filling an audience with inspiration. It's the person on the pitch, leading the charge against a wall of opposing muscle.

But is this what leadership is really all about? Because if that were the case, then regardless of our aptitude for leadership, very few of us would ever be in a position where we had the opportunity for leadership. If, by definition, a team can only have one leader then most of us will never achieve that position.

Most of us are destined to follow, merely because the odds are stacked against us. And here we can see our definition of a leader – its the person who rises to the front despite those odds. The person who isn't promoted or pushed into 'taking charge' but the person who steps forwards and says, "Let's do it – who's with me?" As William Shakespeare's character Malvolio said in Twelfth Night, "Some are born great, some achieve greatness, and some have greatness thrust upon them." If leadership is 'thrust upon' you, are you any less of a leader?

The age old question of whether leadership is born or bred is like the question of the chicken and the egg. Born and bred are the same thing, because we are all born leaders, and we all face moments in our lives that provide the backdrop for our natural leadership talents to emerge.

Scott says, "I believe that in business, in sport, in anything in life, everything you do is based out of your early years. If you change jobs, like moving from rugby to motivational speaking, you're drawing on skills that you created in your first few years. When you're young, you create the engine that powers you for the rest of your life, but once you've created that engine, it can power anything that you choose to do. If you make a change or even take a break, then after a bit of tuning, your engine is ready to go again, it's always with you.

I'm a great believer in putting in a huge amount of work to start with. Learning what's right, what's wrong, working, building, training, and then at the end of it that's why professional athletes, when they come to the back end of their careers don't have to train that much.

The muscle memory's there, the understanding is there, you fine tune what you want, you realise what works, you realise what doesn't work. Sometimes you put a little bit more fuel in the engine, and then bam, off you go. That's because of all the hard work you put in before.

The hard work that you put into developing your skills as a leader always pays off and you never forget what you've learned. This is the engine that powers your career and allows you to reinvent yourself as time passes. The people who have been most successful are the ones who have reinvented themselves so that they've always got something new to offer and something new to keep them interested.

If you're not dedicated to what you're doing, how can you expect anyone to follow you? So focus on the things you loved to do when you were young, the things you were best at. While you might not carry on doing those specific things, what you'll find is a set of common themes which define your 'engine' and keep your focus and your commitment strong."

Leadership isn't something that you do, it's the engine that you've created to power your focus and commitment, it's the passion which inspires others to follow you.

In almost 30 years of working with leaders in business and the media, Paul has seen a whole spectrum of leadership styles. "I've seen autocratic leaders, dictators, servant leaders, hard leaders, soft leaders, passive leaders, dynamic, collaborative, inspiring, uninspiring, leading-from-the-front, leading-from-behind, you name it. When people try to define leaders, they often think of only the charismatic guy, standing at the front of the room, saying something worthy and inspiring. I've found that real leaders aren't really like that. The stereotypical image of a leader is a PR image, it's good for the TV cameras and the press conferences, but in reality leadership is about pursuing the vision, not bragging about it. Real leaders are more likely to be found in a back room, helping to plan out new products or campaigns, talking to the people in their business and, most importantly, talking to customers. A real leader doesn't just tell others what to do, they do it themselves. They walk the talk, they lead by example.

They devote their time to what makes the biggest difference, and that usually involves connecting with the people who are vital in delivering their vision.

Some of the most inspiring, compelling leaders I've worked with have been the quietest. They know what they need to do and they get on with it. They don't think in terms of inspiring or motivating people, they know that people will follow if they choose to. They would rather have people who engaged with the reality of the work than those who are hooked by a good PR campaign and want to hang on their coat-tails."

If you're starting your own business then it's perhaps more likely that you're doing something that you're personally committed to. But what if you're in a corporate management role? How can you create that passion for widgets or financial services? You can't fake it, you can't pretend to be passionate about a new range of vending machines. I'm sure you've seen corporate mission statements that try to convey something exciting and fail miserably because it's totally implausible that anyone would care that much about whatever the company produces.

If you're a corporate manager then you're expected to show leadership skills, and you might even be sent on leadership training courses. But as we said, leadership isn't something that you do, it's the set of qualities that inspire people to follow you, and those qualities will be different depending on the situation and the people involved. There simply isn't one kind of leader for every situation.

What's the secret, then, when you're not in an exciting, fast paced, do-or-die environment? It's so simple that you must have worked it out already.

You're not leading widgets or mission statements. You're leading people. Those people depend on you guide them to success so that they can do rewarding jobs in a well-managed team. They rely on you to create a safe environment where they can do their best, try out new ideas and learn from their mistakes. Your passion, your 'engine' is what enables you to inspire those people, no matter what their jobs are.

Remember that you're leading people - they rely on you and you rely on them

THE LEADER'S STORY

One of the most important things that a leader has is a story. The leader's story is the reason that people choose to follow. It's the narrative that runs parallel to your own life, something that you relate to, something that gives you the courage to follow.

Do you have a story? Or do you just have goals, or sales targets, or a corporate mission statement. Do you really think such narrow, trivial statements will give people what they need to push beyond their limits? Look at the successful brands and businesses around you today. How many got there through sheer luck or knowing the right person at the golf club? The only secret to success is determined, focused hard work. Persistent, tenacious, never-give-up hard work.

A rugby captain's story isn't "Let's win the game". What does that even mean? We already know that victory in a match is short lived. Where does it take you? What does it add to your story? How does it draw followers and supporters in? How does it lay the foundations and pave the way to success, whatever that means?

"It's about the jersey, and it's about understanding that you only ever pass through this life", says Scott. "When you're passing through this life, and when you play for Wales, you only ever pass through the jersey, you don't ever own the jersey, you're lucky enough to wear it. I watched my father wear it, I watched Mervin Davies, watched Phil Davies, watched Evan Lewis wear that jersey. When I go and put that on, it's almost like the empowerment from all those people. There is a little bit of that in the jersey."

Who would have thought that a rugby shirt could be part of that story? Because that shirt outlives any player, the shirt itself is a symbol which tells a far greater story than any one player.

"When you finally hand that jersey over to somebody else, you just want to make it a little bit better than when you got it. I think that's the important thing is to understand where you've been, what you're doing, and the future as well. Why are you doing it? That's the great thing. When I see a new player running around in that jersey now, and making it his own, it's just the best thing in the world. There's a little bit of me in that jersey somewhere. It's just fantastic."

When you look at your job or your business, can you say the same? Can you see your legacy? Can you see how you have contributed a few lines to that story.

No doubt you've seen leadership experts, maybe even retired sports stars, talking about the leadership vision but even a vision is short lived and is really just a fancy name for a goal. A story, a true-life, gripping, edge-of-seat narrative is far more compelling, and it's your story that your followers choose to buy into, because they want to be part of that story. They don't want to be on the sidelines, they want to be in the thick of it, right there with you, because your story becomes their story, a story that they can tell when they say, "I was there, I was a part of something special."

Scott says, "Do you know the best thing about history? Creating it. In School of Hard Knocks we create history. Never ever take it for granted because you get to make history in the next five minutes, and you get to make it better than it's ever been before.

Although the story's about me, I have to make it about them. If you can do that, then you can catch an audience.

It's exactly the same if you do a speech, or if you play a game. Preparation, preparation, preparation. If you go and give a speech, and you know what you're going to talk about, it may manifest seven different ways. Things ebb and flow within the speech. Things ebb and flow, things go right, things don't go right.

On the pitch, because there is an opposition, you've got to react to what they're doing as well. You're going to try and manipulate them to what they're doing offensively and defensively. The muscle memory, the training, all the preparation you put in place, hopefully then becomes automatic. If you can do that and it becomes automatic, then you can be like the top players in the world. People say, 'They seem like they've got so much time on the ball'.

That's because the preparation you've put in, and the number of hours you've put in, people only see the end result of that. They assume that you have some special talent or gift, but they don't see the hours of work you've put into getting where you are.

A second in a rugby match is like a lifetime. You do things, and you see things, and the ball just comes in and that becomes automatic. The more authenticity you can get into a game, the easier the game becomes, and as well in business. The more you practice, the quicker you make decisions. The quicker you make decisions, the easier the decisions become. The quicker you make it, the more you perceive it is the right decision."

Paul often works with business leaders who seem to procrastinate over important decisions, however that's not really what's happening. "A leader will seem to delay making an important decision, and his or her team will get anxious or frustrated, they'll say that the leader is wasting time, or procrastinating, or delaying, or even putting off the decision. What I find is that, in most cases, the leader isn't putting off the decision, they're actually trying to put off the consequences of that decision. In fact, they already know what they want to do, but they feel very uncomfortable with the impact on other people. Maybe the decision affects jobs, or the performance of the business, or a number of important relationships. The leader knows what they must do, and yet they can't bring themselves to do it. The behaviour appears as indecision, but it's actually inaction. Of course, the real problem is that the leader is taking too many conflicting needs into account instead of doing what they believe is right and then working to make that decision work."

As Scott said, "The quicker you make your decision, the more you perceive it is the right decision."

"It's a fine balance between a decisive action and a hasty reaction, and actually that's the key. If you're reacting, you're not in control." says Paul. "Once leaders realise what they're doing, the obvious question is, 'how do I know if I'm acting or reacting' and to answer that, you need to take a step back and look at the bigger picture.

If your current decision is in response to your present situation being interrupted by something that has happened outside of your control then you're reacting. If your current decision is in response to your goals and to feedback that you have not yet achieved those goals then you're acting.

This doesn't mean that you shouldn't react, only that you should consider your response to external events rather than letting them dictate your actions."

How you act, react and respond tells people something about your personality, and that becomes part of your leadership story. A quick-to-act leader has no long term advantage over a considerate leader. However a leader who knows what to do and fails to do it will struggle to inspire confidence in his or her followers.

The decisions you make leave a trail, and that trail becomes your story. Over time, you will develop a reputation for being a particular type of decision maker – ruthless, or compassionate, or hasty, or considerate, or... what? As you look back through your own story, what characterises your decisions?

You might be wondering what is so important about decisions and why they're part of your leader's story. Firstly, decisions mark turning points, and those turning points define the route that you take as a leader. Your decisions will be remembered by those who follow you as the times that something changed, and change is what we are all attuned to.

Secondly, because decisions lead to change, your followers will remember how they were treated in those times of change. There is no 'right way' to behave, it's just that your consistent behaviour will attract followers of a certain kind. If you don't like the followers you're attracting, behave differently.

There are really only two ways that you can fail in this. You can either make decisions for other people rather than for yourself, or you can be inconsistent in how you approach decisions.

If you make decision to please or impress others, you're second guessing what's important to them. They are grown-ups, they can make their own decisions and they are responsible for their own actions. If they don't like what you do, so what? They can do whatever they want and leave you to do whatever you want. On the other hand, if they approve of your decisions, so what? If you are working for their approval, you are not following your own path.

Inconsistency usually shows up under pressure. Under normal circumstances, you might be a democratic leader, asking the opinions of people involved and considering different points of view, yet under pressure you might lock yourself away and bullishly pursue your own interests. This inconsistency directly leads to mistrust, because your team knows they can't rely on you. When you're under pressure, you're more likely to be acting out of fear, and as much as you don't like to admit it, your true nature is showing. Don't hide from it or deny it, embrace it. Even the most selfish leader will be followed by people whose goals align and who can see a benefit from working with someone so single minded and determined.

The personality of a leader is really no indicator of success and it really does take all sorts. Of course, a quiet, democratic leader is unlikely to last long on the Rugby pitch, but in the boardroom there is much more space to accommodate different personalities.

All of this combines to form your leader's story. Where you came from, where you are now, where you're going. All of these show your followers the journey that you're on, and the right people will want to share that journey with you.

YOUR TEAM

Do you know what they call a leader with no followers?

Just a guy taking a walk.

If you're trying to play alone, you're not a leader. Just a player or an entrepreneur perhaps. It sounds so obvious to say that a leader needs a team that we often overlook the unique relationship between the two.

How do you relate to your team? Are you 'in charge', expecting them to follow your instructions? Perhaps you see yourself as a 'servant leader', leading by supporting. You might even believe that you are collaborative leader, working with your team, at their side every step of the way.

There is no right or wrong way to lead a team, because every type of leader will attract and create a team which ultimately complements the leader's personality and style. What does matter is that, within your team, the members are treated as equals to each other.

"It doesn't matter who is in your organisation", says Scott, "they're all as important as everybody else because it doesn't matter whether it's your multi-million pound player, or your medical staff, or your water boy, or – it doesn't matter who it is. All command the same respect. Because once you lose respect from one part of it, then it can then become a stone rolling downhill. It picks up more and more speed, but then at the bottom, you're out of a job. That's why I think that in dealing with people you've got to treat everybody equally to gain that respect. I think the more you do that equally, the more respect people get off you and the more likely they are to come to you with their problems as well."

You can't command respect, though. You can't force people to respect you. And, most importantly, no-one is ever going to respect you for your job title, your qualifications or school tie. They are only ever going to respect you for the way you treat them.

People are only ever going to respect you for the way you treat them

"A good leader pushes people in the direction they think that they're good at." says Scott. "I promoted a player to international captain of a rugby club. Not because I thought he was the best addition. Not because I thought he was the best player on the team, but I thought it would improve him as a player because he was a bit unruly. He was a good player for us. He was a big man. He had a lot of yellow cards. The actual responsibility made him a better player, made him more responsible as a player, and everybody around him tried to help him. By doing that, it brought the team closer together, and made him more aware and made him come out of his shell.

I think what's important is understanding people, giving responsibility to people who might not believe themselves they can do it, but you see something in them. I think if you do that, then you can nurture people to become whatever, whether it's rugby players, or with golfers, or tennis players, or business leaders. The only reason people have coaches and leaders are to get the best out of people. If you do that as a leader, as a coach, there's no better feeling in the world."

A leader cannot exist without a team, and the relationship that you form with your team is therefore critical to your success.

Here's an exercise for you. Take a blank piece of paper, or use the space provided here, and draw two circles, one to represent you and one to represent your team. Do that now.

Once you've done that, come back to this book and consider the questions that follow.

Don't look at the questions until after you have drawn the circles.

Leader on the Pitch

Are the circles touching or not? Why?

Do the circles cross over or are they apart?

Is one circle inside the other? Why?

Which circle is bigger? What does it mean?

Which circle is higher? What does it mean?

Which circle is on the right? Why?

What does all of this tell you about your relationship with your team?

What does all of this tell you about your relationship with the person you follow?

What other relationships *could* you have drawn?

What does this all tell you about yourself?

How do you feel as you consider all of this?

This exercise is simply a mirror. If it reveals anything which is new to you, I guarantee those new ideas won't be a surprise to your team. A mirror shows you, not only what you already knew was there, but the exceptions too, the food in your teeth, the spot on your nose, the hair out of place. Other people knew about your faults long before you did. The more often, and the more carefully you look in the mirror, the more likely you are to see yourself as you aspire to be.

Your team is a mirror too. If you've lost your connection with them, that's unlikely to be their fault, no matter what you say to fool yourself. If your team aren't delivering results, is it because they're stupid or ineffective or that they make mistakes? Or is it more likely that you're not explaining

Leader on the Pitch

yourself efficiently, or that you're not clear about your vision, or that you're not connecting with your team effectively?

In other words, if you don't like what you see, is your mirror to blame?

Your team is not just a means for you to execute your plan, they are also your feedback mechanism, your eyes and ears, your senses that will inform your ability to navigate towards your vision.

Paul's experience of helping leaders to form and communicate their vision spans decades, and he sees the same issues cropping up again and again. "When a leader talks about their vision, they can have a tendency to think only about what they want and forget about the people who will deliver on that vision. They also have a tendency to assume that the situation will evolve according to their plan. The problem is, of course, that the various people involved have free will and are likely to misunderstand, misinterpret and make mistakes. Customers and competitors won't behave as expected and the political and economic environment will change. If the leader doesn't use her or his team as a feedback channel, they will be unable to respond to these changes. The effect will be that the team is stretched further and further between reality and the vision, and the pressure on them will be compounded by the leader's frustration. All in all, a leader who doesn't listen has next to no chance of achieving their vision."

At the end of the day, you can't do anything alone. Obviously, you need clients and customers, and you need supporters, and suppliers, and a whole team of people who depend on you and want to help you.

Scott needed a team around him to support him through injury in 1997. "I got injured in a test match, smashed my knee. I couldn't give up, and I set myself a challenge. My dad played the test match, my uncle played the test match, my godfather played the test match, so I said to my wife, "Nicola, I want to play on the Lions Tour in 2001. I want to play the test match." I said, "I want to play the test match." We said great, how are we going achieve it? I took a 45% pay cut to go back and I failed my medical because my kneecaps were in two and I had arthritis in my both knees, and the doctors said no. Luckily, Gareth Jenkins called and said, "You know what it's like; you'll be fine."

The doctor told me a year later I needed to stop playing because of my knees. I said, "I can't stop playing; it's the only thing I can do." He shoved silicone injections into my knees. I have more silicone in my body than Pamela Anderson. Then, I could only run once a week. I could only play on a Saturday, train maybe on a Thursday or Friday. The rest of the week I would work in a pool.

Then, in 2001, I got that letter saying "Congratulations, Mr. Quinnell, you are selected on a 2001 Lions Tour." The biggest thing for me was when I scored a try in the 2001 Lions Tour game against Australia in the first test.

If you've ever seen it, I just get over the line, and I just look up, and I just nod my head.

That was just a little thank you to everybody who achieved my goal.

When I'm talking about achieving personal goals, I look back after that game, and I look back at the doctors and the physios. I look back at my teammates. I look back at my family, I look back at everybody who allowed me to achieve that one personal goal in 4 years, and it took over 250 people. If they hadn't come together, if I hadn't said to Nicola, "I want to play for the Lions," and she hadn't supported me, and the doctors hadn't supported me, and the coaches hadn't supported me, and the players hadn't supported me, there's no way I could have scored that first try in Brisbane in 2001.

If you don't ask for help, who's going to give it to you? Nobody comes and says 'let me help you'. You have to ask, 'can you help me?' The biggest thing that I learned was the fact that if you've got goals, tell people because that gives you a conscience. If you ask people for help, you know what happens? They help you. That is the biggest thing for me, and that's why I tell kids in school if you're struggling in school, just ask for help because you'd be surprised how many people just want to help, but what they need to know is what's wrong in the first place."

Over 250 people helped Scott to recover from his injury and realise his dream of following his family tradition.

How many people are helping you to achieve your goals? And have you asked them for help yet?

YOUR PITCH

The word 'pitch' is an interesting ambiguity, both of which are very relevant here. On one hand, your pitch is your playing field, your arena within which you play out your leadership role. On the other hand, a pitch is a method of communication, designed to influence an audience.

As a leader, you must master both.

Assuming that you are an expert in your own business, you know the rules of your own game. You know the environment within which you operate. You know the legal, economic and regulatory environment within which you can operate your business. You know the constraints of your people, your products and your resources. You know what you can achieve and you know what you can change. What's most important within all of this is that you know yourself.

Do you really know yourself? I'll guarantee that you don't. You kid yourself that you do. Paul works with many professionals who are convinced that they're communicating clearly, and that the problem is that other people aren't listening. "How many people have to ignore you before you start to realise that you might not be saying anything that they can hear? It's such a common problem because we only see the outside world, we never see ourselves. We see photos and reflections, yet we never see ourselves as others see us. How can we? So we have to rely on other people as a source of feedback, to keep us on track."

Maybe you've had the experience of spending hours working on an important presentation, perfecting every detail, only to find that it simply failed to hit the mark. Maybe you didn't get the job, or the investment, or the board approval for a new project. You only have to watch an episode of TV's Dragon's Den or its international equivalents such as Shark Tank to see one entrepreneur after another deliver what is in their mind a smooth, seamless, watertight pitch, only to be pulled to pieces on the most obvious of omissions. The pitchers spent so long polishing their shoes that they forgot to calculate realistic profit projections. Actually, they spent so long polishing their shoes to distract from the fact that they *knew* their projections were unrealistic.

Here's the very essence of what you must focus on when you are preparing your pitch. Authenticity. You simply cannot fake it. No self-help guru can teach you how to stand and walk and talk like an authentic leader. You either believe in what you're doing or you don't. There is no middle ground.

On the Rugby pitch, Scott knows that an opposing player will absolutely recognise any hint of doubt or hesitation and take advantage of it. "When you're running down the pitch, the moment you think whether you should go left or right, faster or slower, you might as well stop and hand the ball over. The other players will be all over you. You think you're looking for an opening and you get so focused that don't see how that distraction affects the way you're running, your confidence, your commitment. Your opponent will take advantage, they won't hesitate to punish a mistake."

In business, your opponents are not waiting to punish your mistakes. You are not that important. But in that moment's hesitation, the world will continue to turn, with or without you.

"When you pick a point on the pitch, just go for it. Never stop, never look back, just keep going. Your decision to make that run could be right, it could be wrong, you can't know that until you're at the other end. Your run ends when you're where you want to be, and if you stop to think, that's where you want to be and someone else will take the ball from you. You'll be lying in the mud, wondering what just happened. Pick your target and go for it."

The most important thing to remember about your pitch is that it is *your* pitch, no-one else's. No-one else can deliver it for you. If you write a script and give it to someone else, it has to become *their* pitch, because they are not you. Giving other people your scripts limits them and it limits you.

In Paul's book 'The Pitching Bible' he describes the seven secrets for a successful pitch, and this might be a good time to share a summary of those with you.

1: It's All About Them

You have your own reasons for what you're doing and why you want to lead. Whatever those reasons are, you have to remember that they are not, in themselves, good reasons for anyone to follow you. They are only the reasons that you want something, not the reasons that you deserve it.

Any decision is an investment in the future. Therefore, just as with any other investment, you have to present the projected return on investment for the decision maker.

Your pitch should not be, "I want, I want, I want"

Your pitch must be, "You get, you get, you get"

In short, while you are pitching because you want to achieve an outcome, the pitch is ultimately for the audience's benefit and it's them that you have to focus on. Think of everything that you're going to say from their point of view. Is it going to get the right message across to them?

Taking time to clarify what your goal actually means to you is the most important step you can take. How many times have you put effort into achieving something, only to discover it's not even what you wanted? Or perhaps things changed along the way and you hadn't revised your goal?

It's easy to think that you know what you want, and in fact we are so used to not even thinking about our goals that we all assume that we know exactly what we want. However, when you really sit down and explore your goals, I guarantee you'll find angles that you hadn't considered before.

Paul says, "When I deliver pitching training to companies, I ask what the team in the room know about who they are going to pitch to, and I am often surprised by how little they know about their audience.

I was helping a team in a TV broadcaster prepare for an important pitch. I came in two days before the pitch and found that they knew next to nothing about the person who was going to say yes or no to the programmes they were due to pitch.

To prepare for the day, I called a contact in the business. It took me about 20 minutes. It took the people in the room about 20 seconds to exhaust their knowledge of what they knew about the man who was about to make or break their careers for the next two years. When they fell silent I told them everything I knew about the man. Former jobs, likes, dislikes, marital status, kids, hobbies. Then, to stress my point I showed them that within hours of first hearing his name, I had connected with him on LinkedIn and Facebook.

The pitch wasn't about what the team wanted to sell, it was all about him."

2: It's Already Too Late

When does the pitch start?

Most people say that the pitch starts when you show the first slide, when you stand up to speak, or even when the recruiter walks into the room.

In fact, the pitch starts the moment the audience buys the ticket; the moment that the audience first commits to listening to your pitch. That is the point at which their expectations start to form, and that is the point from which you must be able to influence them.

Whether you're pitching to potential investors, employees, business partners or clients, the scene that you set before you stand up to speak is vital. Whoever you're pitching to, they will have expectations and preconceptions. They are judging you long before you open your mouth. Whether it's through your invitation, or your phone call, or even through social media, every one of those communications that you get right makes it twice as easy when you're standing there, ready to deliver your pitch.

But what do I mean by 'getting it right'? I'm not talking about being perfect, or reading the audience's mind. I mean that you put in all the effort that you possibly can, you present yourself in a way that is true to yourself, and you don't skimp on the details.

Advertisers have, for many years, used the acronym AIDA when designing advertising campaigns:

☑ Attention – get the person's attention

☑ Interest – hold their interest

☑ Decision – get them to make a decision

☑ Action – get them to take action

It's certainly worth bearing AIDA in mind when you're designing your pitch, because you really need to plan your pitch to drive the Action, not the Attention. By the time you're standing there, you already have the audience's attention, they're already interested and they've already made a decision to invite you in. Your pitch is the 'call to action'. They have already shown a level of commitment to you, now it's time to act.

3: Steady, Ready, Pitch!

The audience has to be ready to listen before you start speaking. Get their attention and get into rapport with them, but avoid ice breakers, because they actually distract from the topic of your pitch and break rapport. Most obviously, an ice breaker works when there is ice. Why would there be ice? Why would you assume that it's going to be difficult or awkward to open your presentation?

Many people say that it's important to be in rapport with the audience, so here are some key points to remember about rapport.

Don't

☒ Stand behind a barrier such as a lectern

☒ Give all your attention to one person

☒ Turn your back on the audience

☒ Talk to the slides or whiteboard

☒ Hide in the corner

☒ Argue with objections

☒ Hide your true intentions

Do

☑ Let your audience see you

☑ Give attention to everyone

☑ Face your audience

☑ Acknowledge objections

☑ Smile

☑ Pause before beginning to speak

☑ Make eye contact

☑ Be honest

☑ Get close to the audience, but not too close

☑ Nod

☑ Keep smiling!

While it would be nice if everyone you pitch to is straightforward and reasonable, it's an unfortunate fact of life that some are not. For some, it's just the way they are. Others like to play the game of 'good cop, bad cop'. While it doesn't do their own reputation any good, you mustn't let it get in the way of your message.

Whether someone genuinely disagrees with you or is just being disagreeable, here's a simple checklist to help deal with the situation. If you hear something that you disagree with:

✔ Pause

✔ Notice how interesting it is that someone could have that point of view

✔ Say, "Yes, and..."

Leader on the Pitch

In the art of improvisational comedy, performers are taught that disagreement kills the conversation dead, whereas 'Yes, and...' keeps it alive and fosters creativity.

Overall, remember to pause and take as long as you need to prepare yourself. Your clients would rather hire someone who takes a moment to prepare for an important event than someone who rushes in and then flounders half way through for lack of preparation. All good leaders know that time invested in preparation is time well spent, so you send the right messages just by pausing before your pitch!

4: Dream The Dream

Your vision, was created in a dream world. In order for that to become a reality, you need to draw the audience into that dream.

Drawing the audience into your dream with rich, vivid, emotional, sensory language allows you to convey far more than you ever could describe in facts, figures and 'benefits'. Bring your pitch to life and let your words carry the sights, sounds, feelings, tastes and smells of success.

Stories bring your vision and your pitch to life in a very powerful way. If the conversation is relatively unstructured, you can illustrate any example of a goal or achievement with a story.

However, just telling a story of an achievement isn't enough, you have to bring the story to life with the right emotions. You're not just telling the story to inform the audience about the facts of the situation, you are aiming to influence how the audience feels about the story so that it conveys the right meaning to them.

When you're talking about your aspirations, either for yourself, for your team or for your customer's business or venture, you can use a strange quirk of language to emphasise the emotional connection.

When people talk about good things, they talk about them in a certain, consistent way.

> **Good** memories are
> **big**, bright,
> colourful, **close**,
> sharp, **vivid** and *moving*.

The same goes for bad things.

> **Bad** memories
> are small, dim,
> dull, far away,
> fuzzy and still.

Which do you think is best suited to your leadership pitch?

5: Mind Your Language

While 93% of your message may be conveyed non-verbally, there is no doubt that your language conveys the raw information that your audience needs to make a decision.

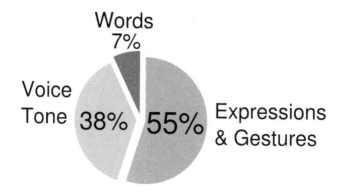

You already know the importance of conveying not just facts to an audience but feelings and meaning.

Fact + Emotion = Meaning

Listen to the people around you and the stories they tell; about their weekend, a meeting they've just been to or a project they're working on. Listen to the way that they tell the story; the words that they emphasise, the expressions on their faces. Notice how they are trying to influence how *you* feel by communicating how *they* feel. This is the natural process of empathy, but it is also being used to manipulate your feelings about an event.

The famous research illustrated by the pie chart on the previous page shows that the overall meaning of a message is made up of three components; the words that the speaker uses, how they sound and how they look when they speak those words. A lot of people dispute the percentages, saying that words must of course make up the majority of the meaning. For example, "Hello", cannot possibly mean, "Can I have a banana?". That would be ridiculous. Oh, wait, unless you just got home from the supermarket, your friend walks in, looks at the bananas you've just unpacked, and says, with eyebrows raised and a hopeful smile, "Hello...." With that voice tone and expression, your friend could use any one of a hundred words, and the meaning would be the same.

By concentrating on how you feel about an event or achievement as you tell the story, your non-verbal communication will naturally and automatically convey the meaning alongside the words that you choose.

If someone asks you to talk about your business or your leadership vision, they are inviting your pitch and they will have formed their own expectations and preconceptions based on what they already know about you. However, an unsolicited pitch makes it much more likely that you have to get the listener's attention (remember AIDA) and overcome any cynicism on their part, caused by their 'WIIFM?' filter. Examples of this would be the cliched 'elevator pitch' where you want to make the most of a chance meeting with someone.

The WIIFM filter allows you to ask "What's In It For Me?" whenever you're presented with a fact or decision. You might also experience this as the "So What?" filter, the "Why Should I Care?" filter and the "Don't Tell Me What To Think" filter.

When you're meeting new people at a conference or networking event, or even at a sports match, you're potentially changing the subject by talking about whatever you want to talk about, especially if the event has a social purpose.

Our 'WIIFM?' filter allows us to evaluate incoming information and judge it against our own beliefs and perception of the world. It protects us from accepting other people's beliefs too readily, and it prevents us from accepting new information too.

Luckily, you don't have to fight your way past the 'WIIFM?' filter, as there are two simple forms of communication which will bypass it completely.

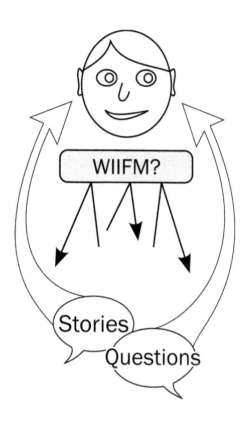

Questions

Questions are a powerful way to convey new concepts by building on the listener's existing knowledge. A question bypasses the listener's 'WIIFM?' filter. However, for the listener to make sense of the question, they must accept whatever it presupposes.

For example, what have you found to be the most valuable part of this book for you?

This question presupposes that the book has more than one valuable part, that you find it valuable and that you have already realised that value.

We hear questions when:

- The speaker's voice pitch rises through a sentence

- A sentence starts with a word such as why, when, where, how, what, which, who etc.

- A statement ends with a tag question, such as couldn't it, don't they, do we, can it, etc.

Asking questions during your pitch can be a very effective way to ensure the listener gets thoroughly engaged in the decision process.

Above all, someone who talks continuously, ramming their virtues down the audience's throat, will never get far.

An old adage in sales is that 'telling is not selling', and good sales people don't have the 'gift of the gab', they have excellent questioning and listening skills.

"Telling is not selling"

By listening, you get to find out about the person you're pitching to. In fact, the head of a media agency said to me that his best sales people are the ones who learn to be 'on receive' while they are pitching to clients.

Even when you're pitching, you can still be listening, judging how the audience is responding to you and adjusting your pitch accordingly to make sure you get across the message that you intend.

Stories

We don't communicate using factual statements alone; they are linked by a narrative, which includes characters – who did what to who – and a sequence in time, so that we can recreate the situation mentally. Imagination is a close substitute for the real thing, and even John Lennon said,

"Reality leaves a lot to the imagination". Stories are the gateway to the fundamental process of human learning.

As one person is talking, anyone listening is translating the words back into the original sensory experience. Of course, they can't translate it into exactly the original, so they are substituting their own experiences and references in order to make sense of it.

The person listening to the story puts themselves in it.

As they empathise, they 'get the message'.

"I get the message"

What does this mean for you?

For a start, it means that the more narrative you use, the easier you are to listen to.

Secondly, it means that the richer and more emotive your language, the more accurate the pictures are which you create in your audience's mind.

Narrative communication – storytelling - is vital, it's natural, and you already have a lot of experience in using it:

✔ Anecdotes

✔ Case studies

✔ Reports

✔ Any description of an event

It's interesting that the practice of competency based interviewing, used to make the interview process consistent and objective, relies entirely on your ability to tell relevant stories which have the right words in; words that tell the interviewer how you analysed a situation, how you took action and how you reflected on the result that you achieved. Having a selection of appropriate stories will definitely put you ahead of the pack.

If you struggle to tell stories coherently, or if you feel that the point you want to make gets lost in the details, you can use the well-known STAR format to structure your stories.

Situation	The background
Task	The task or objective
Action	What you did about it
Result	What you achieved and learned

Make sure you focus on your own actions, not those of the group you were in. The audience doesn't want to hear what other people did, they want to know about you.

This is especially true if you are pitching for finance, investment or even crowdfunding. Yes, you need a good idea and a sound business plan, but ultimately, any investment is a risk and your numbers are guesses. The question is, how confident are you? Do your investors believe that your numbers are realistic compared to your ability to do what you say you're going to do?

A global head of HR told me that, in answer to the question, "how would you sum yourself up in one word?", one candidate once replied "messy". Guess what? She didn't get the job. As a leader, describing yourself as a 'maverick' or a 'creative person who isn't bothered with details' may not give them confidence in you.

The stories you tell, and your overall leadership story, give your investors and your followers confidence in you, so give yourself a reputation to live up to.

6: Say It Again, Sam

No doubt you have heard the presenter's adage, "Tell them what you're going to tell them, tell them, then tell them what you told them". Get your message across in as many different ways that you can, and realise all of the different communication channels that you're not using; the way you dress, the way you walk into the room, what you say in your invitation and your pitch itself all communicate your intention, and when all of those factors are aligned, you multiply the power of your message.

A good way to ensure that your pitch is memorable is to follow this checklist.

- ✔ Make your pitch as short as possible, but no shorter

- ✔ Have a single compelling reason for the audience to follow you

- ✔ Open your pitch with that reason, then provide all the supporting evidence, then conclude it with that same reason

- ✔ Use words and phrases that the audience already associates with you, or has a sense of familiarity about

- ✔ Ask for the audience to take the action that you want

7: The End... Or Is It?

Every rock star understands the importance of an encore. It's the thing that most concert-goers rave about. Some performers make the audience wait for up to an hour before being reluctantly coaxed back onto the stage for one more song... or two... or ten.

I wouldn't expect an audience to be shouting "More!" at the end of your pitch, but they will certainly be feeling it.

If you're pitching for some kind of support or investment, or to potential customers, clients or partners, then as an absolute minimum, you must send a follow up letter, reminding them of the most important points that came up during your pitch, reiterating how much you want to work with them and reinforcing the return on investment that they'll get by working with you.

There are two very important points to always bear in mind about follow up letters.

1. Just sending a letter, the same day as your pitch, shows that you are serious

2. Reiterating the points that you want the audience to remember about you will greatly increase your chances of getting the result you want

If you have good handwriting, make the effort to write your letter by hand on good quality paper. In our digital world, it leaves a wonderful impression when someone receives personalised mail that someone has clearly taken some time and trouble over.

Many years ago, a colleague of mine had an interview with an Internet company that represented his dream job. After the interview, he hand wrote a letter to the interviewer, thanking him for his time and reminding him why he should hire my colleague. My colleague got the job, and in his first week, people were saying to him, "Ah, *you're* Fred, it was *you* that wrote the letter!" The hiring manager had apparently been running up and down the office, excitedly showing people the letter.

I was telling my son about the importance of 'thank you' letters for his birthday and Christmas presents. He said "I know, Dad, you've been telling me about it ever since I was born!" I realised that I was preaching to the converted when he went upstairs to his bedroom and brought down the four already completed letters in his best 11 year old handwriting. "There you go", he said. "I realised years ago that if I sent a thank you letter, the next birthday or Christmas, the person always sent another present!"

Sam also pointed out to me that he had bought his mother a fountain pen and some lovely writing paper for Christmas so that she could "write thank you letters to her customers so that she will get more business and we can go on more holidays" The apple doesn't fall far from the tree!

Top Tips for a Leader on the Pitch

It's All About Them: Give your audience what they need to make the right decision.

By The Time You Start, It's Already Too Late: The pitch begins the moment the audience starts thinking about it.

Steady, Ready, Pitch!: Get the audience's attention before you begin.

Dream The Dream: Share your intentions by sharing your emotions.

Mind Your Language: Use questions and stories to bypass the audience's critical filter.

Say It Again, Sam: Repeat and emphasise the messages you want the audience to hear.

The End... Or Is It?: Make sure you follow up, as quickly as possible and with specific reference to the key points.

YOUR OPPONENT

Take a look in a mirror. Do it now. Not just a glance. Not a cursory check to see if your hair is how you imagined it. Take a good, long, hard, careful look.

You are looking at your opponent.

By the laws of physics, the reflection you see is already in the past. Your self image is even more out of date. And your reputation? Well, that precedes you, as you know.

Scott has spent his career learning about his opponents. "I used to love hurting other people, so the less I hurt, the more they hurt, the more chance I've got of winning the game. There's only one place in the world that bullying is acceptable, and that's on a sports field. Ultimately, that's what you're doing. You're two clans, you're two sides, you're two – it doesn't matter what you call it, you are trying to beat the opposition.

By trying to beat the opposition, you've got to get one over them, you've got to be bigger, you've got to be stronger, you've got to be angrier, you've got to get in that mindset. That's why when you play a rugby game it takes 24 hours, I think, to prepare yourself to play a game.

My wife used to tell me, on a Friday night that if we are playing, it would start when I'd come home from work. I would gently get into that mode where on a Friday night I'd have spaghetti bolognese, and then I'd have some sweets after, and then I'd go to bed at a certain time, I'd get up in the morning, then I'd have beans and toast, then I'd put the kit in my bag the right way, then I'd get to the game. I'd have my massage an hour before. I'd put my lucky pants on. Everything has its place 24 hours before the game.

That 24 hour process is actually allowing you to turn into somebody else who can do something that, if you did on a street, you'd go to prison for. When you cross that white line, you can't instantly turn it on at game time. Training you can, you can just turn it on, but in a game, because you've got eight guys who want to hurt you as bad as you want to hurt them, you've got to become somebody else. It takes a process and a mindset to be able to do it.

Fear is the catalyst, it gets you to do something which is brilliant. It inspires you, puffs your chest out, gets you to breathe the fire, it can feel absolutely fantastic, or you could be a shrinking violet. You can become this absolute monster, or you can just go home. People use fear in different ways. People who can become huge when they're motivated by fear might shrink away at other times. It's about the mindset. The top three inches of your body, your brain, it's the strongest muscle in the body. It's the most powerful tool that you've got in your armoury. If you don't believe you can win, you ain't going to win."

Paul has studied business leaders who are able to 'switch it on' in the way that Scott describes. "Henry Ford said, 'Whether you say you can or you say you can't, you're right.' To learn to switch it on, find out what great athletes, like Scott, do. When you talk to great athletes, what are they doing? What are they saying? They'll say. 'You just felt in the zone' or 'You felt everything was going right'. Does fear go away because you are in the right place in your head? What's happening first? You'll feel the fear and go one of two ways, either you'll want to run away or you'll tackle it head on. Well, guess which is going to get you what you want?"

But how do you take the fear and focus it on the challenge you face? Scott suggests one way of stacking the odds in your favour. "Who you surround yourself with makes a huge difference. If you surround yourself with positive people, who support you, who say, yeah, we can do this, then you'll feel supported, you'll feel like you're at least heading in the right direction.

Surround yourself with positive people

The people who say 'what if?' in a negative way, 'what can go wrong?', they can put doubts in your mind. It's the 'what-iffers' who can make you lose your confidence.

At the same time, you need people around you who aren't afraid to tell you when you're about to do something stupid, something maybe driven by your ego or your need to prove something. If you can't be honest with yourself about why you're doing what you're doing then you'll be stuck on one side or the other, you'll always charge head on, or you'll always run away. You won't be able to tell the difference because you're not doing it for yourself.

We've all been motivated to prove a point, to win an argument, maybe to prove something to a parent or a teacher who doubted you.

But you can't do it for them, and that's a tough thing to face up to because we all want to think we're in the driving seat, and most of the time we're not.

'What if?', it's only two words, but it totally changes your mindset. You've got to get the 'you-willers' around you. The 'what-iffers', try and get away from them. An individual sport, I suppose, is slightly easier because you're in control of what you want to do. Although you have a big team around you, I think that in a team sport, you've only got to get out of bed the wrong way, and you've become a 'what-iffer'."

Of course, in business, you are very much playing a team sport. Even if you see yourself as an entrepreneur, you still need partners, customers and a market environment to work within. You even need your competitors.

Without competition, there is no choice, no freedom. You might think that life without competitors would be easier, but in fact you would stagnate. You would have no comparison, no benchmark, and no incentive to improve. You only have to look back at the nationalised industries of the 1970s to see the effect of a monopoly.

It's so tempting to worry about your competitors and what they're up to, so always remember, your greatest competitor, the only opponent you ever have to worry about, is the person looking back at you from the mirror.

The only opponent you ever have to worry about is the person looking back at you from the mirror

Leader on the Pitch

THE RULES OF THE GAME

Every game has rules so that all players know how to play the game and what behaviour is, and is not, permitted. The rules of the game serve a far more important purpose, though, both in rugby and in business. When each player knows the rules, they will make their own decisions. They won't look to their colleagues or the referee, they will instantly know that what they are doing is right.

However, knowing the boundaries of the game is not enough. That doesn't tell them how you want them to play the game. You've already addressed that in your pitch to your team.

When your team know the rules of the game and have aligned themselves with your story, they will each make their own decisions, their own individual choices. Like a shoal of fish or a flock of birds, they will appear to be acting as one, as if through some telepathic link. None exists, they are simply each following the same, simple rules.

In any game, there is an incentive for following the rules, which usually comes in the form of a penalty for non compliance. You want to pick up the ball and run? That's no problem. You just don't belong on a football field. Players are free to do whatever they want, as long as they do it somewhere else. Your own rules are no different. If you want your team to play as a unified team and one player wants to make himself the superstar, how do you deal with that? Do you sacrifice the integrity of the team for the sake of winning the match? How do you know that a unified team would not have won the match anyway? You can't turn back the clock and play the game again, so what you do, what we all do, is look for evidence that supports our decisions and prejudices, even when those decisions might be harmful in the long run.

We all want to be treated as individuals, yet we also each want to feel part of something. We want to be treated fairly, and that means being treated equally compared to everyone else, even though we want special treatment. We want to be the same and different.

As a leader, you have to create rules which are fairly applied for everyone, and you have to act on those rules. If you're running a business and one person persistently arrives late for work, you can't turn a blind eye. If you do, everyone else will see what you're doing and think, "Why should I work so hard? Why should I turn up on time?" No matter what you say the rules are, the rules will actually adapt to the minimum standard you're prepared to accept. If you accept poor timekeeping, poor workmanship, poor customer service, those will be your rules, despite what you say you want and what you say is important to you. What you say will have an effect for a while, but if you're inconsistent, what you do will have a much longer lasting, and hard to change impact.

What kind of rules should you have? Well, the first place to look for inspiration is your own sense of what's important to you because if you can't follow your own rules, you can't really expect anyone else to.

On the Rugby pitch, with a small team and a clear objective, the impact of a disengaged player is huge. Scott and Paul both had to deal with this challenge during the filming of School of Hard Knocks, as the participants sometimes struggled to find their own motivation to be there. Scott says, "At the end of the day, you can only play with the people who turn up to training. All of the lads were accepted and wanted to take part, but some of them found the early mornings and the cold wet weather for training too much. They found it easier just to stay in bed or go back to whatever they were doing. We're not going to go chasing round for them, they either choose to be there or they don't. Sometimes the harder ones to deal with are the people who turn up to training but in their minds they're somewhere else.

You can try and motivate them, get them involved and hope they pick up the pace, but sometimes you have to tell them to sit it out for a while and get their head together."

Paul adds that, "In every series of the TV show, we have had people who have taken longer to adapt to the discipline. One of the participants in an early series detached himself from the group, and when people do that, it can be because they're scared of not succeeding, or through fear of whether they have the stamina to see things through, or it can be because they resent other people telling them what to do. He needed more than an attitude adjustment, he needed to understand that what he was communicating in detaching himself from people was making his life more difficult and the chances of him getting help were less likely.

He said very early on in the course, "I ain't got the mental strength", and this was a clue to how he was reacting and learning in life. He needed a lot of support to get his head in the right place, and ultimately that's an investment that you have to weigh up, to decide if the person is worth that attention at the expense of the team."

The time to decide on your rules is not when you're in the heat of the moment, trying to figure out how to respond to a crisis. The time is now.

OVERCOMING FAILURE

Never be scared to fail. Failure is essential. Failure is the most important part of the process. Unless you are willing to put yourself in a position to fail, you will never grow. You will never accomplish anything worth doing because those people who succeed are often on a razors edge between success and failure. They are bold. They are unlike other people.

You do not learn much from success. We've both observed that success can actually make you a little bit anxious because things have worked and you're not entirely sure what you did differently on this occasion as opposed to another occasion and suddenly everyone is telling you how smart you are and you're a little bit uneasy.

Whereas, when you fail and you look at something and say 'this just doesn't work', you submit yourself to a really interesting process of self examination, analysis and scrutiny.

Only in failure do you really look closely at how you could improve. Only in that close examination are you able to learn what you really need to learn.

The old saying that 'success is going from failure to failure without loss of enthusiasm' is so true.

To be a true leader is to understand and welcome failure. Without failure there is no learning and therefore no ability to lead.

One of the questions that people ask us both most often is, "What gave you the strength to keep on going? How did you manage to never give up?"

It's a good question, because when we first began our respective careers, we had no idea how to keep going either. An important part of it was the people we surrounded ourselves with, the people who depended on us. Without those people, we could have given up, walked away and no-one would have known.

When Paul wanted to make sure he couldn't back out of running his first marathon, he told forty people close to him in the six months beforehand in order to make sure that he saw it through. Creating your own deadlines is an excellent way to keep you on track but what's more important is that you share those commitments with others. That's not to lay the responsibility or blame on other people, it's to have other people ask you, "How's it going? How's the preparation? Are you nervous?" and so on. It's about connecting your goal with a bigger importance, it's not just about you because nothing ever is. Everything we do is for others, and depends on others. We're part of a network.

It's easy for people to say, "You just find the strength, because you have to". That's not very helpful when you're facing resistance to your business project or sales program.

Have you ever thought you were lost because you didn't recognise the road you were on? Perhaps you were trying to follow someone's directions, and you were driving further and further, thinking, "this can't be right". You're at the point of turning back and, suddenly, you come round a bend and you recognise where you are, or you can see your destination just ahead. You breathe a sigh of relief that you didn't turn back, and you tell yourself that you knew you were on the right track all along.

Of course, there are also times when you are completely and utterly lost, and you should have admitted it a long time ago.

One of the traits of a great leader is therefore not just to never give up, but to know when to give up and when to persevere.

Any fool can put their heads down, ignore the warning signs and carry on regardless. In the corporate world, that can result in wasted time and money. Corporate history is full of 'white elephants', projects that consumed valuable resources and yet were destined to fail.

There are equally as many stories of people who gave up when they were moments from victory.

A leader must consider the impact on their team. of giving up When the team has chosen to follow the leader's vision, they have committed their own time and energy to your project or cause. They expect the going to get tough, and they know that they are going to have to pull out all the stops, and they are willing to do that because they believe in your vision. What happens when they see you give up on that?

When you give up, you double the disappointment that your team feels. When

Leader on the Pitch

you persevere and don't succeed, the team is disappointed of course, but they know that they pulled together and followed your lead and, most importantly, they know that they each made a choice to follow you. When you stand by your vision, they know that they made the right choice, even if things don't quite work out as you planned. When you give up, they can feel misled, betrayed and even embarrassed.

Just as every member of your team made a free choice, you also need to remember that you made a choice to embark on whatever it is you're doing. Making a choice makes you responsible. It puts you in control.

Fear is everywhere, and what's important is how you use that fear. This is very much on Scott's mind when he's on the Rugby pitch.

"The fear, to me, is transferred into adrenaline. Adrenaline is transferred into positive energy. Positive energy turns into outcome. As long as you can channel that, and you can express the fear, and you can go into it and face it, there's no better feeling at the start of the game.

That's the only part I miss of rugby. I don't miss the playing any more. I don't miss the training any more. I do my own type of training. I miss that buzz in the changing room before the game. I've said it before, when you get those butterflies, the closer you get to the game, the bigger, the stronger they get. If they're not there, then there's something wrong. I'm not getting that feeling on the Rugby pitch any more, I'm getting it when I stand up in front of 2000 people and talk about my story.

If you don't feel that fear, that energy, then it's time to give up, I think. It's the positivity of turning that fear into something wonderful. The fact that when those butterflies, when those nerves come, I think that's when you get the best of yourself because complacency doesn't set in. There's nothing better than standing on the edge of that cliff the first time that you're going to do something new, to push yourself.

As soon as you do it, the adrenaline pumps through the body. It's just the best feeling in the world. I think that's why we go around the world chasing it.

Sometimes the fear can be not wanting to fail, and when you go out there, and things don't work, or the game doesn't go well, or the speech, you go out there, and it doesn't quite work. It's adapting and knowing that you can go and do it again, but maybe do it slightly differently.

That's why comedians go on warm-up tours for six months to get enough material to do a two-hour show. People see the two hour show; they don't see the six months in the build up. You can't be frightened to fail, and failure means success in the end because you learn, you hone things. Unless you risk failure, you learn nothing and you have no new material, or fresh ideas, or whatever it is for you.

Sometimes I stand there when things don't quite go well, or I'm on live television and I say something I shouldn't say. Afterwards, I just think, "Ha-ha, I can't believe I just said that. It's brilliant!" Don't be frightened to say something because if you never say anything, you never make any mistakes. The only way to never make a mistake, to never fail, is to do nothing, to stay home, stay safe. And you have to ask yourself which is more important for you.

The first time I ever stood up and did a presentation, I remember getting into the venue and not eating. I couldn't eat my food before I spoke. They said, "Don't you eat?" I said, "No, no, I'll be fine." Now, I have three course meals. I mean, I probably stop off and have a sandwich before I go and have a three-course meal. People say, "Don't you get nervous?" I say, "No." Even though sometimes I am, you have to put everybody else at ease because they're looking to you, they're almost waiting for you to tell them how to feel, to show them that everything's going to be fine."

Paul tells his clients to "Look forward to things going wrong because that is when you have the most fun." The psychological effect of 'looking forward to things going wrong' reframes the idea of failure, because it's only when things don't turn out how we expected that we really discover what we're made of. So many companies brag about how great their customer service is, but in reality you only ever discover their quality of service when something goes wrong. Every customer is happy when things are going right!

We've both experienced, first hand, the importance of connecting with the audience before a presentation – getting to meet people, chatting, building rapport, so that when the presentation begins, there is already a bond, at least with a number of the people in the audience.

Scott adds, "The way I see speaking is very similar to how I played rugby - all the training is done beforehand. Everything, you train, you do automatically. My best speech is when I wake up in the middle of the night and I think of something. I do the speech in my sleep. Then I get up the following day and then just do it. I suppose it's because of my reading and writing, the fact that I couldn't read and write for so many years so everything I've done is in my head.

What sane person stands up in front of 2,000 people and just talks? Nobody, no normal person would do that. You'd shit yourself. That's normal! Basically, when you're up there, all the training you've done then manifests itself in a speech. I can very rarely remember. If you ask me at the end of an hour speech, what I've talked about, I haven't got a clue. It's there. I've heard myself before, so there's no point listening to myself. I know it all. I just focus on the audience, who are they, what do they want to hear. It's all about them[1], as Paul often reminds me.

When you've rehearsed to the point that you know exactly what word to say at what time and you know when to let the audience laugh then that's not a presentation any more, that's just a monologue. You might as well be talking to an empty room. As soon as you put people back into that picture, you

---

1   See the chapter 'Your Pitch'

have to connect with them, you have to find a way to relate with them, and that means you can't predict what's going to happen because you need them to be involved too. If you're the kind of person who wants to control every move, you're going to struggle unless you give them all a script and tell them when to laugh, when to clap and so on. If you've got to control everything, you're only going to get yourself stressed. You have to know where you're heading and get the audience to go there with you. Most of all, you have to accept that you might fail, and that's OK, because you'll learn the most from that.

If you go and you do a speech, and you know what you're going to talk about, it may manifest in different ways. Things ebb and flow within the speech. It's exactly the same, whatever the field, things ebb and flow. As you go on in business, things ebb and flow, things go right, things don't go right."

Athletes mentally rehearse before an event, but they don't rehearse the game, they only rehearse the pitch or the track. This is notably the case in track sports such as motor racing, cross country skiing and so on where you're simply moving too fast to react, and the only way to reach the end of the track is to anticipate every twist and turn before you get there. What these athletes don't do is rehearse what the other competitors will do. When the racing driver imagines the track, there are no other cars on it, because on the day of the race, he can't control what those other drivers will do. The only thing that he can do is to know the track inside out and then he can focus

Leader on the Pitch

on the other drivers without wondering if a bend is coming up.

Paul appeared regularly at London's Comedy Store for many years, and even after hundreds of performances, that mental rehearsal was still important. "We were performing improvisational comedy when that style was in its heyday, through the 1990s. The audience was mostly made up of visitors to London, tourists attracted by the Comedy Store's location and reputation. We could have done the same show every night, who would have known? That's the rut that a lot of performers get into, they forget that there's an audience there. It doesn't matter whether it's a new audience or the same one, when the performer just goes through the motions the performance loses its edge. A new audience can see that just as much as someone who has seen the show a dozen times before. So you might think that a performer can't really plan for that, and especially for the improvisational work that we were doing, how can anyone rehearse when they don't know what suggestions the audience will come up with? Well, as a minimum, we knew what time we'd start and finish. We knew the audience would be asked to make suggestions, characters, relationships, places, that kind of thing. And we knew that we would improvise scenes around those suggestions. So we could rehearse, both physically and mentally, for those constants, the things we knew would happen. Then, on the night itself, we didn't have to stop and think what we were doing next, we could be in the moment, involving the audience, playing on their laughs, enjoying the spontaneity, and every show was exactly the same as every other, and at the same time, totally different and unique."

In the game of Rugby too, one pitch might seem pretty much the same as every other. They're the same size, the white lines are in the same places, and while each game is unique, experience tells Scott that his opponents will tend to behave in certain predictable ways. "Ultimately, because there is an opposition, you've got to react to what they're doing as well. You're going to try and manipulate them to what they're doing offensively and defensively. The muscle memory, the training, all the preparation you put in place, hopefully then becomes automatic. If you can do that then you can be one step ahead of the other team. Some of the top players in the world spend a lot of their training time working on this, understanding the other team. People say, "Oh, they seem like they've got so much time on the ball" and that's because they've put the preparation in, they're one step ahead because they've put the work in beforehand."

When you put the work into your training and preparation, people only see the few minutes that you're performing for them. Whether that's on a Rugby pitch or in a board room, that's all people see, and they will think that it all comes naturally.

"That's because the preparation you've put in, and the amount of hours you've put in. If I said to you now, "Pick up your coffee cup", how long is that taking you? It's instant because it becomes automatic. By the time you've thought about it, it's gone to your brain, and you've executed it, it takes a second. When you're on the pitch, you don't have time to stop and think.

A second in a rugby match is like a lifetime. If it becomes automatic, and you do things, and you see things, and the ball just comes in, comes past, then that becomes automatic. The more authenticity you can get into a game, the easier the game becomes, and as well in business. The quicker you make decisions, the easier the decisions become. The quicker you make it, the more you perceive it is right decision."

Be certain that what you are doing is worth persevering with. You need to make sure that you can still remember why you're doing it, and that you're still doing it for the right reasons. Just take a moment to think back to the decision that you made to embark on this project or journey. Be honest with yourself, were you doing it for yourself or for someone else? What did you hope to gain from it?

Every goal has to have some personal gain in it. No matter what that gain might be, it's certainly easier to keep going when you know exactly how you will benefit. Perhaps the best personal benefits include self respect and the knowledge that you succeeded in spite of any setbacks, because ultimately, when you find the strength and courage to keep going, what you overcome is not any external obstacle. What you have overcome is your own doubt.

When you think back to why you're on this path, you might also think about other times in the past when you have proven yourself to be right, so that you can remind yourself of what worked for you.

Remember, too, that when you give up once, you make it far more likely that you will give up again next time. When you begin to rationalise or play down your surrender, you make it acceptable, and that is most certainly not acceptable. If you decide that it is better to stop and turn back, you will ideally feel bitter disappointment, because you have made a decision based on insurmountable external obstacles. If you have to rationalise the decision to turn back, you're soothing your conscience and trying to make yourself feel better. Your doubts have won, and you must never allow this to happen.

By reminding yourself why you started on this particular journey, you recommit to it. It's important to keep communicating this to the team too, reminding them of what it is that first inspired them.

All too often, people get so bogged down in the details and minor setbacks that they lose sight of the overall objective that was the original source of their enthusiasm. Since your team are probably going to be much closer to those details and setbacks than you are, it is vital that you keep that inspiration firmly in their minds.

I'm not saying that you should be blindly confident or plough on regardless, thinking that if you ignore the obstacles, they'll go away. The reality is that you have much work yet to do. What you're doing is reminding

Leader on the Pitch

yourself and your team of why it's all worthwhile.

An important part of making a commitment to your goal is to burn your bridges. If you set out on a difficult project or journey with a plan B in the back of your mind, you are giving yourself an excuse, a way out, before you have even started. You make it easier to go back. This is not the same as a lifeline, because a lifeline gives you a way to return to a safer position so that you can try again. A lifeline is a way to make it safer to achieve your goal, whereas a plan B is a way to give up on your goal.

Make public commitments, get sponsorship, even write yourself a mission statement and pin it to your wall. Make sure that, when you succeed, it's for you and when you give up, you have everyone else to answer to, including your team. These public commitments are a sign for them too.

In building such a high level of commitment to the vision and goals of the team, it is important not to lose sight of the steps that lie immediately in front of you.

Break the overall objective down into realistic steps. Don't think in terms of breaking the objective down into easy steps though. How many houses have you been to where the owners tried to make their renovation project easy to achieve by doing a bit at a time? They end up in a bigger mess than they started with. When you break down the objective, make your steps logical and thorough. Plan short term goals that keep you moving and keep you focused on what you can achieve, right now. When you plan those short term goals properly, you can occasionally step back and see how much closer you are to your end objective.

Encourage your team to do the same, and ensure that you regularly review progress with them and celebrate every step forward, not with incentives and prizes but with sincere recognition and appreciation. The team are making progress because they want to, not because there is a gift voucher in it for them.

In sharing every success with the team and supporting them through the everyday obstacles and setbacks, you will no doubt find that they have ideas to share about the project or cause, and it is vital that you take their feedback from the front line and use it to make your own decisions. Again, this is an aspect of being responsible for your vision.

Other people are full of good advice. Some people tell you what you want to hear, some offer enthusiastic encouragement and some can come up with endless reasons why your project is doomed to failure. Ultimately, most people will tell you what they would do if they were in your shoes. They are not in your shoes.

If you solicit advice, be careful that you aren't only asking for the advice that you want to hear. If you're thinking of giving up, you might only listen to the negative advice. That might convince you that it's better to give up, or it might make you want to prove them wrong. Ultimately, in your heart, you know exactly what you need to hear in order to get the motivation that you want.

Never ask a committee to make a decision for you. Remember the old saying, a camel is a horse designed by a committee Never give up your control and your choice. This is your journey, your goal, and you must think for yourself. Your team will definitely want to know that their voices are heard and that their feedback is important to you, but they also need to see you making your own decisions. Yes, they will want to make tactical decisions about how to achieve a task, but what they look to you for is strategic decision making, decisions of direction and intention. Your ability and willingness to make these decisions is another way of letting your team know that you believe in your vision.

By all means, gather information. But in the end, weigh it up for yourself. You can gather all the information that you want, it probably isn't going to change your decision, but at least you can honestly say that it has been an informed decision.

When you have negative thoughts, which are natural and normal, it's good to catch them and acknowledge them. You don't have to sit down and have a heart to heart about them, you might diffuse them with some humour. The important thing is that when you have a negative thought, keeping it to yourself amplifies it and before long it becomes your new focus, your new goal. When you have a negative or destructive thought, say it, express it, exorcise it. Be very careful not to do this in front of your team, though. They may not always be able to tell the difference between shaking off negative thoughts and the warning signs of you giving up.

Scott has worked with people in many walks of life who were ready to give up. "With the dyslexia, I worked with a lot of people who are incredible. Sometimes they can't read. Sometimes they can't write. Sometimes they lack self-esteem. Sometimes they're the type of people who will be in a job maybe for ten years. I call it the invisibility cloak syndrome. They sit in the corner, they put an invisibility cloak over their head. They do what they need to do in a day, and they'll go home. They're so frustrated because they know they're capable of doing a lot of other things. They know they're capable of being better than they are.

Because they put these huge barriers around themselves to make themselves feel comfortable enough, the worse thing in the world, they sit in the corner. Those people have a massive benefit to the company and they need just a little bit of encouragement. I speak to so many people who say, "I felt like after ten years I want to help, but I'm frightened to help." I say, "You're not frightened to help. You're frightened of making a mistake."

They say, "I haven't made a mistake in ten years" and I tell them, "I know - and because you haven't made a mistake in ten years, you haven't learned anything in ten years."

Fear of the unknown is one of the emotions that drives the young men who take part in

School of Hard Knocks. Paul reflects, "It's interesting because obviously we worked for a good few years with people who've never played rugby, and we have to deal with the fear element of rugby. If you've come to rugby late, and you've never had to go and charge at another man, that's a big step. We use that, obviously, as a stepping stone to say, "Look, if you can do that, you can do anything." What do you think, for instance, companies could learn from that overcoming fear ethos, pushing yourself to that level?"

Scott adds, "I think it's the fact that, a lot of the time, if you go into a company – I sold chemicals with my Dad for years, and if I'd go and knock on somebody's door, I'd say, "Excuse me, I sell chemicals, industrial water treatments. Would you like to buy some there?" They say, "No, fuck off," and you say, "Oh, thank you very much. That's very kind of you. Thank you very much." I go to the next one and I say, "Excuse me, sir, would you like to buy any?" "No, fuck off." "Oh, thank you very much. That's very kind of you, sir." I say to the third one, "Excuse me, I sell bleach. Would you mind if I sell you something?" They say, "Oh, yeah, come in and we'll have a talk."

What's the one you remember? What you've got to remember is that the more doors you knock on, the more opportunity you've got of walking through it. Never be frightened. My daughter works, she sells chemicals now, and she comes back some days and says, "Oh, this woman was really rude, she told me where to go," and I say, "Did it affect you?" "No, I just went and sold two to the person next door." That's what you've got to have in life – the ability to keep going and focus on the times when things go your way. The more doors you knock on, the more success you're going to have."

It's too easy to lose focus and momentum because you feel you aren't making the progress that you want. It's good to be ambitious, but, if you're not realistic, your perceived lack of progress can quickly sap your energy.

When you step back, literally stop what you are doing, take a physical step back from the situation and think through the reality of where you are and what you are doing. Look at yourself as a stranger would. Don't judge whether what you're doing is good or bad, don't judge if you're as far forward as you ought to be, simply look at where you are right now. Knowing precisely where you are means that you will find it much easier to find your way to your destination.

When you think about some of the things you have achieved in the past, you can see that your current situation is easily within your capabilities. You can see not only where you need to be but also how far you have come.

Of course, you still need to be realistic. When you step back and look at the reality of your situation, you can also see a realistic way forward for you. Planning for setbacks doesn't make you pessimistic, it makes you realistic.

If planning for setbacks makes you feel that it's not even worth trying, you're being pessimistic. If planning for setbacks makes you find alternatives and gives you more determination, you're being realistic.

However you see the bigger picture, the system that you are a part of and the network of people who rely on you, you can understand that you are where you are right now because of the choices that you made, and that means that you are in control of your situation and your destiny.

Whether you decide to give up or carry on is your choice, and by making it for the right reasons and based on all the right information, you will always be in a better position to lead others.

Paul concludes, "I've heard so many leaders paraphrase the NASA quote and say to their teams 'failure is not an option'. Not only is it a terrible cliché, it's not even true — failure must be an option if you are to learn and grow. In fact, if innovation, growth and learning are your goals then failure is your only option! Failing is not important, what's important is what you learn and how you get up to fight another day."

Failure must be an option if you are to learn and grow

CELEBRATION

As an effective leader, you will find that your team will go to the ends of the Earth for you. But what happens when they get back? And what do you do if someone makes a mistake?

How you celebrate failure and success is the final piece of the puzzle.

Leaders don't only celebrate 'big victories', they celebrate anything and everything that represents a step in the right direction. That celebration could be anything from a full-blown awards party for the team to a simple 'thank you' or 'great work!' because celebration is a form of recognition and you'll get more of what you give recognition for.

A celebration isn't just a reward, though, so most of the time you won't be giving away flowers, chocolates and nights on the town. Most of the time, you are celebrating in order to reinforce your rules and gently shape the team behaviours which will deliver your vision.

You may think, "I hire people to be good, why should I give them recognition for doing their jobs?"

The answer is simple. You hired them because they have the skills, capabilities and experience to meet your requirements. But why they continue to get out of bed, day after day after day and support you? That's because they feel valued, they feel part of something important, and the way you show that you value them is through frequent recognition. Catch them doing something right and they will get it right more often.

Paul has worked closely with many household names in the business world and has had the opportunity to observe many of them in action. "The leaders who are best known and the most successful all have something in common – the ability to make people who work for them feel good. Delivering praise, a kind word or a pat on the back at the right time means that people who work for them are loyal and consistently go above and beyond what is required by their job description. Great leaders make their workforce feel valued and special. Not through big shows, which are more about the leader's ego than the team's performance, but through genuine and most importantly, personal thanks."

You might want to go out for dinner and drinks after work – not only when you've completed a key project or landed a big deal, but because you want to create a team spirit and a mutual understanding. You wouldn't do this every week because people have their own lives, but every few months is enough time for your team to get to know each other and create connections that go beyond the confines of the 'day job'.

If you're working from an office, you can set up a notice board where you post 'thank you' letters, customer feedback, success stories and so on. You might even do this via social media. What's important is that this is a public display of what you value in your team. If you value customer service, you'll display testimonials. If you value financial results, you'll display sales data. All too often, leaders say they want one thing but publicise another, which reveals their true intentions and erodes trust. A leader who says he cares about his team but shows that he only cares about results is not going to create an atmosphere where his team want to go the extra mile.

If you only value results, say so. Recruit people who want to deliver results. Publicise results. Don't be afraid of who you are, walk the talk and attract the right people into your culture. And yet, still remember to recognise and celebrate those results. Your team don't deliver because hitting a target is its own reward, they are motivated to hit that target because of what they expect to get in return.

A vital way to give recognition is to simply listen to, and value, the ideas that your team come up with.

"In leadership, listening is so very important because otherwise how would you learn? If you don't listen, you don't learn. And most leaders are so used to thinking they're always right that they've forgotten how to listen.", says Scott. "I would always learn, and would always look at new ideas. The great thing about listening is getting the right answers out of the people that you put in place. That's the important thing - getting the people that you've put in place in business, or in your social group, or in your team that have like-minded ideas, so when they come up with ideas you can say, 'That's a fantastic idea, I think we'll do that.'

You empower them, and you empower yourself. First of all, yourself, because you've put the right person in place. Then you have to trust the people you put in place. They are a part of the leadership group. It's very difficult, in a way, to hand that trust over, but the earlier you do it, the more successful you're going to be."

We all want the same things out of any team that we're part of, whether it's a personal relationship, a business or a sports team. We want to contribute, we want to feel that we're part of something bigger than ourselves, we want to be treated fairly and we want to feel valued.

The easiest way to achieve all of that is to listen.

Paul works with business leaders on their communication skills, and usually those leaders start by thinking that the skill they need to develop is talking. "Leaders, sales people, executives, entrepreneurs, they all think that successful communication is about what they say. They think that if they could speak with greater impact or influence then they would be more successful. Actually, the opposite is true. I've noticed that the more someone talks, the less credibility they have. What we judge people on is, of course, their actions.

However, whilst taking action does communicate a great deal about you, it's unlikely to influence your audience right now. Being able to influence with respect and honesty, putting your point across concisely, having solid facts to rely on, presenting those facts in the way that connects most strongly with the audience, these are the cornerstones of a solid pitch, and you can't do any of these effectively if you don't listen. You begin by listening to your audience's needs, listening to their comments and objections, listening to their interests and buying signals. If you're not listening, how can you ever tailor your pitch to your audience? And how can you know if you're on track?"

Listening to your followers is vital for your success as a leader, and not only does this give you important information, it also serves as a form of recognition. In any relationship, we have a deep desire to be listened to, to be heard. People get frustrated and shout because they don't think they're being listened to.

Your followers will look to you for guidance on what to do and how to do it. If their efforts go unnoticed, if they feel you're not listening, they will quickly become disengaged and their performance will fall. You can offer all the perks and gifts you like, but as you well know, if you forgot your partner's birthday or a special anniversary, no amount of money spent on a gift makes up for it.

Genuine thanks and recognition, catching people doing things right and activities that bring the team together – that's what creates engagement, builds teams and delivers results.

Leader on the Pitch

Catch people doing the right things and give them recognition

THE FUTURE

A leader does not rest on their laurels. With a winning team, the leader's focus is always on the next deal, the next project, the next game, the next season. If you're leading a team then you must have some idea of where you're heading. Planning the future is therefore critical for you to maintain the momentum you've built up so far. Once your team is performing at their best, they don't want to stop. Of course, planning for the future is not just about your team's development, it's about yours too.

Corporate employees expect a career path. More than ever, they expect to be developed, to be nurtured, to be promoted, to be challenged.

What's your career path? If you're an entrepreneur, what's your plan? Higher and higher turnover? Sell your business and move onto something else? What if you're a corporate leader? What's the next step for you?

As a leader, it's easy to think that you've reached the end of the road in terms of career development, that the only move left for you is a bigger business, a more challenging goal.

Scott and Paul have shared this experience in filming School of Hard Knocks. Paul says, "There's no doubt that we're investing in the future. So the young men we work with every year might not literally be the next Pitch Doctor or International Rugby Captain but they are our legacy as much as our own children are. We've invested a part of ourselves, our knowledge and experience.

We've planted seeds, and not all of those seeds will mature, that's their choice. But if we don't plant those seeds and trust that some will flourish, what's the point?"

Scott adds, "What I love about life, is that every moment, we're creating our history.

I love the fact that you can create history day, after day, after day. A lot of it will never be recognised by anybody. Do you know those memories when you look back in school, or you look back at a day you were on the beach, or you look back at the first day you took your son to play football, or the first day you put skis on and you went skiing, or last year you went skiing and it was brilliant because he was in front of you for first time? That's history. You're creating history every day.

You're creating history every day

Never ever take it for granted because you get to make history in the next five minutes, and you get to make it better than it's ever been before.

It's incredible the fact that, ultimately, you all want to achieve the same goal. Success, whether winning the game on the weekend, winning the league, or winning a big account, is something you share. You've got to understand that a league isn't won before Christmas. A league isn't won in your first year. Sometimes it takes two or three years to build a team. That's why every manager who goes into a football team says, 'I've got my three-year plan'. After six months, he's gone because it looks like he failed – and business is the same.

If you look at it, you go into a business, and again, it comes down to goal setting. It comes down to understanding where you're going to be. It comes down to putting a team together. It's not always going to be a quick goal. It's not always going to be quick games. It's not always going to be instant success. You've got to build, and you've got to learn.

I think that's what I think sport can learn from business is the fact that you're in it for the long haul. You set up a new business. Sometimes it's three to five years before you start making money. In sport, they're all after instant success. Basically, that's all I want to do is manage a professional football club and get sacked because that's where you make your most money. In business, it's about longevity. As well, it's about the team you put around you, and understanding that the team you put around you have family, have friends, have a home, have a car to pay for. As a leader, it's your responsibility to everybody. With me, we own a business; we've got people that we employ, and we're responsible for their families, as well. I think that's what a lot of people lose sight of, as well, is the fact that when you see one employee, you don't see a wife and three kids, that's what you need to look at and think about, the families that you're supporting, not just the people you directly employ.

We talk about sport, and we talk about the player being the best he can be. A lot of the time, you look at the footballers and the rugby players, the family is looked after, as well. Make sure the family is around, the wife and everybody are good, so that mentally they are prepared to play the game that they need to play. They get the best beds when they go to hotels. Make sure they've got the best of everything so that when they get out the park, they perform. Ultimately, that's how you get successful.

I think in business, as well, sometimes we lose sight that we're all human beings."

What are you doing to continue learning, to continue growing, developing? Scott suggests that we can find learning in the most unusual of places. "I'm 43 years old and I am learning to do pottery. Do you know who's teaching me? My son, and he's 17. You don't always look for teachers in the places that you expect to find them. Teachers could come in various forms, various guises, various ages. It's who you identify with, who you can work with and respect."

Ultimately, there is no goal, there is no destination for the Leader on the Pitch. There is only a direction, and a way forwards. As you lead and others follow, you have no way of knowing where that journey takes you. All you need is the drive and determination to keep stepping forwards, every day.

Remember Scott's words - you get to make history in the next five minutes, and you get to make it better than it's ever been before.

We'll see you on the pitch.

THE AUTHORS

Scott Quinnell

Scott was born into a
family of Rugby
legends - son of Derek
Quinnell, legend of
rugby union, and
Madora John, the sister
of Barry John 'The

King', with godfather Merv 'the Swerve'
Davies.

Scott started playing rugby for Llanelli
Juniors at 8 years old and went on to play
Internationally for Wales 52 times and also
played for the Barbarians, joining two British
Lion tours in 1997 and 2001.

Scott now appears regularly on Sky Sports
and is a recurring character in the Sky

comedy show 'Stella'. He has appeared on The One Show, A Question Of Sport, Soccer AM and Sky TV's 'School Of Hard Knocks'.

Scott is a patron of the Princes Trust, Make a Wish foundation and The Welsh Dyslexic Association and is an Ambassador for The School Of Hard Knocks charity.

www.scottquinnell.com

Paul Boross

Psychologist, author, performer, musician, trainer, keynote speaker and expert on "the art and science of getting your message across", Paul is also known as 'The Pitch Doctor'.

Paul regularly speaks at international business and media conferences, trains and coaches business leaders and lectures for the Entertainment Master Class, the executive education programme for media.

Paul is the resident psychologist on Sky's School Of Hard Knocks and has presented and featured on BBC2's Speed Up Slow

Down, ITV's Wannabe and BBC1's The Politics Show.

Paul is a Business Ambassador for The School Of Hard Knocks Charity and sits on the advisory board for 'So You Wanna Be In TV?', a social enterprise committed to increasing diversity in TV and addressing youth unemployment.

Paul is a Fellow of The Institute of Enterprise and Entrepreneurs.

Paul's other books include The Pitching Bible, The Pocket Pitching Bible and Pitch Up!

www.thepitchdoctor.tv

Lightning Source UK Ltd.
Milton Keynes UK
UKOW04f2159111017

310820UK00001B/55/P